These Violent Delights...

[*Romeo and Juliet,* II/vi]

Malcolm Emmons: *Cover Photo, Pages* 7, 10, 11, 13, 15, 19, 23, 24, 25, 26, 27. Emmons and Brockway: *Page* 17. Keith McMillim: *Pages* 3, 21. St. Louis Post Dispatch: *Page* 14. John Vawter: *Pages* 16, 28. Wide World Photos: *Pages 4, 5, 8, 20, 22, 30.*

THE RELEVANT

ME OUTS

TO GO

SHAKESPEARE

Hallmark

THESE VIOLENT DELIGHTS...

[Romeo and Juliet, II/vi]

Selected by
Roland I. Swanson, Jr.

SHAKESPEARE ON FOOTBALL

Blessed are
the peacemakers on earth.

[*King Henry VI,* Pt. II, II/i]

Over park, over pale,
Thorough flood,
 thorough fire....
Over hill, over dale,
Thorough bush,
 thorough brier,

[*Midsummer Night's Dream*, II/i]

Pray that our armies join not in a hot day, for by the Lord, I take but two shirts out with me, and I mean not to sweat extraordinarily.

[*King Henry IV*, Pt. II, I/ii]

Oh! that way madness lies;
let me shun that.

[*King Lear*, III/iv]

He that escapes me without some
broken limb shall acquit him well.

[*As You Like It*, I/i]

O, good sir, softly, good sir! I fear, sir, my
shoulder blade is out.

[*The Winter's Tale,* IV/iii]

It goes much against my stomach.

[*As You Like It,* III/ii]

Pray you now, forget and forgive.

[*King Lear,* IV/vii]

Here is my journey's end, here is my butt
And very sea-mark of my utmost sail.

[*Othello*, V/ii]

His nose is executed, and his fire's out.

[*Henry V*, III/vi]

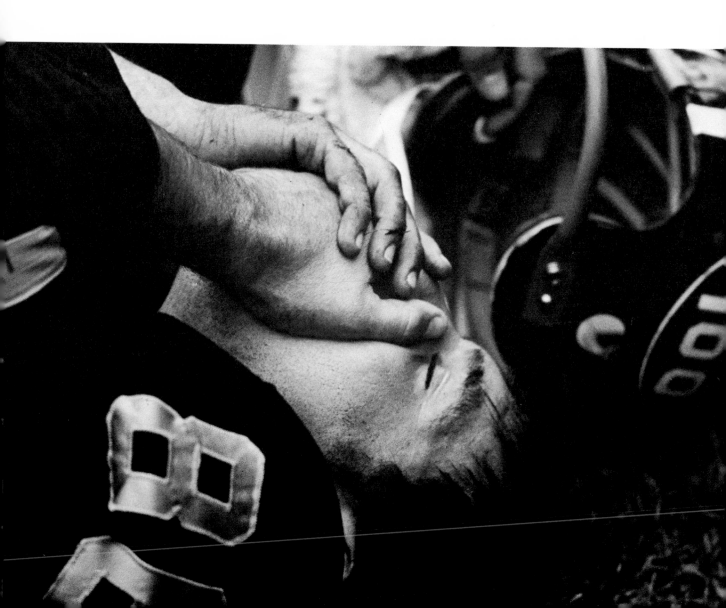

What men have you lost, Fluellen?

[*King Henry V*, II/vi]

I have some wounds upon me, and they smart
To hear themselves remember'd.

[*Coriolanus*, I/ix]

I would be friends with you, and have your love.

[*The Merchant of Venice*, I/iii]

O! Let me not be mad, not mad, sweet heaven;
Keep me in temper; I would not be mad!

[*King Lear*, I/v]

…the sweetest flower
of all the field…

[*Romeo and Juliet*, IV/v]

Chaos is come again.

[*Othello*, III/iii]

...that which they possess
They scatter and unloose it from their bond,
And so, by hoping more, they have it less.

[*The Rape of Lucrece*]

Angels and ministers of grace defend us!

[*Hamlet*, I/iv]

...com'st thou smiling from
The world's great snare uncaught?

[*Antony and Cleopatra*, IV/viii]

...guard thy head;

For I intend to have it ere long.

[*King Henry VI*, Pt. I, I/iii]

Unhand me, gentlemen,

By heaven! I'll make a ghost of him

that lets me....

[*Hamlet, I/iv*]

The play, I remember,
pleased not the million…

[*Hamlet,* II/ii]

These violent delights
have violent ends.

[*Romeo and Juliet*, II/vi]